The Missions of California

Mission San Rafael Arcángel

Jacqueline Ching

The Rosen Publishing Group's
PowerKids Press™
New York

For my parents, Vivien Kiang Ching and Ching Tan, with thanks.

Published in 2000 by The Rosen Publishing Group, Inc.
29 East 21st Street, New York, NY 10010

Photo Credits and Photo Illustrations: pp. 1,4,8,16,21,23,24,30,31,32,33,42,50,51 by Cristina Taccone; pp.5,18,26,39 © CORBIS/Bettman; pp. 7,44,48 © The Granger Collection; pp. 10,13,15, 34,37,38,40 © Michael K. Ward; p. 12 © Seaver Center for Western History Research, L.A. County Museum of Natural History; p. 14 by Tim Hall; p. 17 © Department of Special Collections, University of Southern California Libraries; pp. 20,35 © North Wind Picture Archives; p. 28 © Christie's Images/Superstock; p. 47 © Archive Photos; p.48 © N. Carter/North Wind Picture Archives; p. 52,57 by Christine Innamorato

First Edition

Book Design: Danielle Primiceri

Book Layout: Christine Innamorato and Felicity Erwin

Editorial Consultant Coordinator: Karen Fontanetta, M.A., Curator, Mission San Miguel Arcángel
Historical Photo Consultants: Thomas L. Davis, M. Div., M.A.
                    Michael K. Ward, M.A.

Ching, Jacqueline.
        Mission San Rafael Arcángel / by Jacqueline Ching.
              p.   cm. — (The Missions of California)
        Summary: Discusses the Mission San Rafael Arcángel from its founding to the present day, including the reasons for Spanish colonization in California and the effects of colonization on the Indians of California.
        ISBN 0-8239-5506-0
        1. Mission San Rafael Arcángel—History Juvenile literature. 2. Spanish mission buildings—California—San Rafael Region—History Juvenile literature. 3. Franciscans—California—San Rafael Region—History Juvenile literature. 4. Indians of North America—Missions—California—San Rafael Region—History Juvenile literature. 5. California—History—To 1846 Juvenile literature. [1. Mission San Rafael Arcángel—History. 2. Missions—California. 3. Indians of North America—Missions—California. 4. California—History—To 1846.] I. Title. II. Series.
        F869.M66665C48 1999   99-23212
        979.4'62—dc21   CIP

Manufactured in the United States of America

Contents

The Missions of California

In 1949, architects in San Rafael, California, were given a big job to do. Their task was to build a replica of Mission San Rafael Arcángel, the 20th mission to be built in a 21-mission chain set up along the coast of California between 1769 and 1823. The $85,000 restoration project produced a copy of the mission complex that had once been Mission San Rafael Arcángel. The story of Mission San Rafael Arcángel dates back much further than 1949, however, and it is part of a much larger story—the story of the missions of California.

The Age of Exploration

The story of the California missions began in Spain. In the 1400s, Spanish explorers began crossing the wide Atlantic Ocean to reach a new land. It was a long and dangerous ocean voyage, but the New World, as the Europeans called it, promised a new life. Some voyagers came in search of gold, some came to spread their religion, and some came to escape the hardships or persecution they faced in their homelands.

The Spaniards were quickly joined in their explorations by other newcomers from Britain, France,

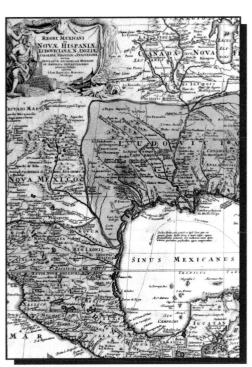

▲ *An early map of Spanish claims in the New World.*

◀ *The restored Mission San Rafael Arcángel.*

and the Netherlands, but the Spanish settled the largest area of land in the New World. They claimed the land that we know today as Mexico and called it New Spain.

When the Europeans arrived in the New World, they met the people who had already been living there for hundreds of years, the American Indians. Some of the American Indians tried to teach the outsiders their way of life, but most Europeans believed that it was they themselves who had the most to teach. One of the things they believed they should share with the American Indians was the Christian religion.

The Spanish government sent friars to set up missions in the New World because the Spanish had discovered that this was a good way to begin settling a territory. Spanish territory spread all the way west to the land that would one day be known as California. No Spanish settlements were built there at first because the Spaniards knew little about this large territory and it would not be easy to get Spanish food, clothing, and other supplies to the area.

Russia's Fort Ross

Eventually, King Carlos III of Spain heard that Russian explorers and fur traders were coming from the north to settle the land. The Russians had been exploring Alaska since 1740. The ruler of Russia had ordered that colonies be built along the coast of the Bering Sea. Russians came to California to hunt sea otter. In 1812, the Russians built Fort Ross on Bodega Bay. There they grew wheat for their Alaskan colonies and traded with the California Indians and Spaniards.

King Carlos III knew California was too important for Spain to lose

Fort Ross was a major Russian outpost in California.

to the Russians. He wanted to keep the land because it was rich, fertile, and near the sea. It was a perfect place to build towns and harbors for ships. In those days, Spanish ships sailed across the Pacific Ocean between New Spain and the Philippines.

The Mission System

It was decided that a chain of missions and presidios would be set up along the coast of California. To found each mission, the Spanish government sent two religious leaders called friars (or *frays* in Spanish) and several soldiers and military leaders. Presidios were military forts for the soldiers, whose job was to protect the missions. The Spaniards

7

▲

A statue of Fray Serra.

had built missions throughout the Americas because it was a good system for taking control of an area and making the local people into Spanish citizens and Christians. Fray Junípero Serra was the first president of the California missions. He founded the first California mission in San Diego on July 16, 1769. Fray Serra and other missionaries wanted to convert the California Indians to Christianity. Indians who were converted to Christianity were called neophytes. The Spaniards thought it was their Christian duty to bring their religion to the Indians. The Spanish government had another reason for the mission system, too. The converted Indians, or neophytes, could be taxed as citizens of Spain, which helped Spain keep its hold on the land. The California missions were built on the best farming lands. The Spanish missionaries did not see the land as their own. They believed that once the California Indians learned the European way of life, the land could be returned to them, although the Indians would still be ruled and taxed as Spanish citizens. Many California Indians were converted. Nevertheless, later events prevented the lands from being returned to them.

From 1769 to 1823, the Spaniards built 21 missions along the

8

coast of California. Soon, small towns grew near or around the missions. More and more settlers came to California. The struggle for control of the territory would last for many years and involve three nations: Spain, Russia, and the United States. For many years, the mission chain gave Spain the strongest foothold in California.

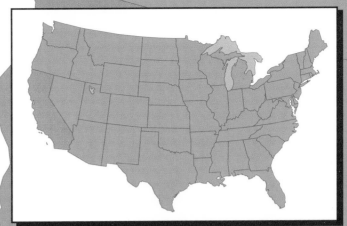

The area where San Rafael is located, between Sonoma and San Francisco, was the focus of much of this international power struggle. It would also be the area where the Americans would later stake their claim on California, during the Bear Flag Revolt.

For the California Indians, these power struggles meant their old way of life was gone forever. Their culture was destined to be forever changed with the introduction of the mission system, and the

○ San Francisco de Solano
○ San Rafael Arcángel
○ San Francisco de Asís
  ○ San José

    ○ Santa Clara de Asís
○ Santa Cruz
  ○ San Juan Bautista
  ○ San Carlos Borromeo del Río Carmelo
  ○ Nuestra Señora de la Soledad

  ○ San Antonio de Padua
    ○ San Miguel Arcángel

  ○ San Luis Obispo de Tolosa

  ○ La Purísima Concepción
    ○ Santa Inés
      ○ Santa Bárbara
        ○ San Buenaventura

        ○ San Fernando Rey de España
        ○ San Gabriel Arcángel

          ○ San Juan Capistrano

          ○ San Luis Rey de Francia

          ○ San Diego de Alcalá

changes and consequences would continue long after the last mission was abandoned.

Life for the California Indians was different from mission to mission. The mission system had both strengths and weaknesses. There were incidents of cruel treatment of California Indians, especially at the hands of the Spanish soldiers who came with the missionaries to build and protect mission settlements. On the other hand, many Spanish friars and California Indians—even though they came from very different cultures—found ways to live and work together in mission communities that were successful both socially and economically. For a time at least, Mission San Rafael Arcángel was one such community.

◀ *The mission system forever changed the lives of many California Indians.*

Before the Spanish

California Indians

When the Spaniards first arrived in California, many California Indian tribes were already living there. There were over 100 different groups, each with its own land and customs, its own language or dialect. The area in which Mission San Rafael Arcángel was

An Ohlone Indian in deer skin to hunt.

built was the home of the Coast Miwoks. Another group of American Indians who would live at the mission were the Ohlones. The Spaniards called them the Costeños, which means the People of the Coast.

Hunting and Gathering

The Coast Miwok and Ohlone Indians were hunter-gatherers, which means they lived by hunting, fishing, and gathering. They hunted game, such as rabbit, deer, and bear. They were clever at building traps and decoys to catch birds and other animals to eat. They also ate wild plants and seeds, especially acorns. The Indians used their special knowledge to take the bitterness out of the acorns and to make them into bread, flour, and mush.

Before a hunt, the Miwok hunter would cleanse his body of smells

California Indians knew how to make the most out of the land's natural resources.

The California Indians prepared food using simple, but effective tools.

that might frighten his prey. He did this inside a *temescal*, or sweat house that produced heat instead of steam. After sweating and cleansing, he would jump into an icy stream. This process also helped him to loosen up his muscles for the chase. Finally, he rubbed his whole body and clothes with mugwort, a plant that smells like mint.

Gathering and preparing food was a social, or fun, part of the Indians' everyday life, because it was during these times that the Indians visited with each other. The acorn harvest was so important to the Ohlone that it marked the beginning of the year for them. They measured time in terms of how many moons had passed since the last harvest or how many led up to the next harvest. The acorn harvest was also a main social event for the Indians. Groups of villages would meet to take part in dancing, trading, and feasting.

Fish was also an important food for tribes that lived on the coast. They gathered oysters, crabs, and clams. Because of this, these California Indians were very good sailors. They built boats from hollow reeds instead of hollowed-out wood. These boats were very light and less likely to sink.

Coastal Indians were skilled at fishing.

Homes

The Coast Miwoks and the Ohlones built their villages along bays or rivers that led to the sea. Outside their villages, they left mounds of shells—as high as 30 feet—from what they had gathered and eaten. These mounds can still be seen today. The hollow reeds that they used to build their boats were also good for making houses.

Beads decorate handmade baskets.

Basket weaving was a skill of the Ohlones and Miwoks.

Trade

The Ohlones and Miwoks traded with each other and with other tribes. When the Spaniards first came, they also wanted to trade with the California Indians. Among the skills of the Ohlones and Miwoks was basket weaving. These baskets were decorated with beads, which the Indians made from olivella shells. These shells were also used as money all over California.

Religion and New Ideas

The California Indians lived close to nature, so nature played a big part in their religion. They believed in spirits that lived in animals, plants, the earth, the sky, and water. The idea of one all-powerful god brought by the Franciscan friars was new to them.

Christianity was not the only thing that the Spanish brought to the California Indians. The California Indians had never before seen mules, horses, or longhorned cattle until the Spaniards brought them to California. The Spaniards gave gifts to the Miwok and Ohlone Indians, such as bright colored cloth, glass beads, and metal crafts. The Ohlones were amazed by these objects. They believed that objects were alive and had their own kind of power.

The Spaniards taught the California Indians about agriculture, which gave them a stable source of food. Hunting and gathering had always been how the Ohlones got food, but they were not reliable sources. The Ohlones had never kept livestock. The Spaniards taught them to raise livestock and to grow their own food.

In the end, the Spaniards found that the Indians of California were not the "savages" that they had expected them to be. Still, they believed that the Spanish culture and religion were superior to that of the American Indians. They believed that the American Indians' way of life could be improved and that they should be converted to

▲

The mission system brought the cultures of the Spanish missionaries and the California Indians together.

17

Christianity. The missionaries believed that they were saving the souls of the California Indians, and the government of Spain wanted to create new Spanish citizens who would work hard and pay taxes.

The Coast Miwok and Ohlone Indians were gentle peoples who welcomed the European strangers with feasts and gifts. The Spaniards did not return their respect or hospitality. These tribes had not built any cities or temples. They had few possessions—even when compared to other American Indians, such as the Iroquois, Pueblos, or Plains Indians. To the Spaniards, all these things were signs that the Coast Miwok and Ohlone Indians were "uncivilized." They watched the Ohlones dig in the ground for their food and called them "diggers."

When the Franciscan friars first came, the California Indians were drawn to them. They were curious about the new ideas and objects that they brought with them. When the California Indians came to the missions, the friars worked very hard to encourage them to be baptized and converted to Christianity. At first, the Indians did not know what this meant or how it would change their lives.

Over time, many of the California Indians would see the Spaniards first as kind spirits, then as harmful spirits, and, finally, as dangerous enemies.

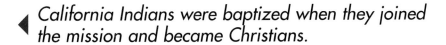

◄ *California Indians were baptized when they joined the mission and became Christians.*

An Unexpected Mission

Mission Dolores

Mission San Rafael Arcángel was begun almost 50 years after the founding of the first mission in Alta (or upper) California. It started as a hospital, and then as an *asistencia*, or sub-mission of another mission. At Mission San Francisco de Asís, also called Mission Dolores, near San Francisco, the California Indians became sick from diseases such as measles, smallpox, flu, and syphilis, brought by the Europeans. These diseases did not always kill Europeans, but they did kill many American Indians, who had never been exposed to the illnesses and had no immunity to them. The area's cold, damp, and humid climate made it even harder for the sick to get better. To escape disease and death, many Indians ran away from Mission Dolores. The missionaries could not stop their converts from deserting the mission.

The friars saw that they needed a hospital. However,

Many California Indians became sick and died from unfamiliar European diseases.

Mission Dolores.

the president of the missions was not so sure how to go about establishing one. There were too few missionaries to staff a hospital, and he did not know who to send to find a place to set one up. Yet it was his duty as the president of the missions to find an answer. His prayers were answered when Fray Luis Gil y Taboada agreed to find a place.

Fray Gil went out in search of a warm, dry spot where sick people would get better. He chose an area that the California Indians called Nanaguanui, located north of San Francisco Bay. Here it was warm, with plenty of sunshine and hills that gave protection from wind and fog. Fray Gil, with the help of Indians and other friars, set up a hospital

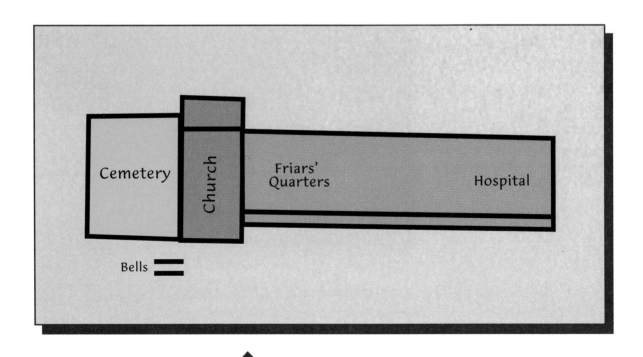

Layout for Mission San Rafael Arcángel.

on that site. They wrapped the sick in blankets and rowed them across the bay to the hospital. In a short time, aided by the benefits of rest and a good climate, the health of the California Indians improved a lot. Word of this spread quickly and other missions began sending their sick to the new hospital.

Mission San Rafael Arcángel

Things were better at the hospital site, which was to develop into Mission San Rafael Arcángel. Not only did the California Indians get well, but mission records show that in its 17 years San Rafael Arcángel gained 1,873 new members. Soon, it also increased its possessions, including sheep, horses, and cattle.

None of this would have happened without the guidance of the missionaries who founded Mission San Rafael Arcángel and the hard work of the Miwok and Ohlone Indians. It wasn't long before the church leaders could see that Mission San Rafael Arcángel was going to be a success.

Livestock was raised at the mission.

The Founding Fathers

Missionaries

Mission San Rafael Arcángel was founded by four Franciscan friars, Fray Narcisco Durán, Fray José Ramon Abella, Fray Gil, and, the man who was then president of the California missions, Fray Vicente Francisco Sarriá. The Franciscans were members of a religious order of the Catholic Church. The Franciscan order continues today. Franciscan friars dedicate themselves to building missions around the world and to teaching others about the Christian religion. Mission San Rafael Arcángel was the 20th mission that the Franciscan friars built on the California coast.

The First Mass at Mission San Rafael Arcángel

On December 14, 1817, Fray Sarriá raised the cross and celebrated the first Mass at Mission San Rafael Arcángel. It was named for the patron saint of good health. Catholic tradition holds that the archangel Raphael was a healer of physical disease. His name in the Hebrew language means "God heals."

That afternoon, Fray Sarriá baptized 26 California Indian children. Indians who were baptized were called neophytes, which meant that they were new to the Christian religion. The friars led the neophytes in song, and Mass was given in both the neophytes' native language and in Spanish. They sang the Te Deum, a Latin hymn of praise, with the Mass.

The Hospital

Because Mission San Rafael Arcángel began as a hospital, Fray Gil was put in charge. He was well known for his knowledge of medicine.

◄ *Like the other missions, San Rafael Arcángel had a Catholic church on the grounds.*

He had other good qualities, such as a caring manner and an ability to work well with others, which made him the right man for the job.

Fray Gil worked very hard to build the mission and to take care of the sick people who went there for help. He also preached about God and spiritual ideas in a way that made the neophytes listen to him. Many new converts from the Coast Miwok and Ohlone Indian tribes joined Fray Gil and his community at Mission San Rafael Arcángel.

Still, San Rafael was not yet a full mission. It was only an *asistencia* of Mission Dolores. As an *asistencia*, it received food and building supplies from Mission Dolores. Any converts who joined San Rafael and any produce grown there belonged to Mission Dolores. It was not until October 19, 1823, that Mission San Rafael Arcángel gained complete independence as a mission.

Fray Juan Amorós

In 1825, two years after Mission San Rafael Arcángel became independent, Fray Juan Amorós took Fray Gil's place. He was so successful at running Mission San Rafael Arcángel that within another three years, the mission community grew from 300 to 1,000 people.

Fray Amorós was a man who took his religious studies seriously. As a missionary, he was very well respected both by other Franciscan friars and by the California Indian neophytes. One Spanish general in California described Fray Amorós as "a model of virtue, charity, humility, and Christian meekness." These were all the qualities in a person that the Franciscan friars admired most. Fray Amorós will always be remembered for making the most of Mission San Rafael Arcángel.

◀ *Fray Gil looked after the spiritual and physical health of the mission's neophytes.*

27

One story says that Fray Amorós carried his lunch in his sleeve. This was usually an ear of dry corn, roasted over coals. He would eat it slowly as he gave directions to the neophytes at work. He was long remembered for his simple way of living.

Fray Amorós traveled among the California Indian villages near the mission to encourage the people there to become neophytes. He covered a lot of territory and, in spite of the possible dangers, he had very little protection with him. He served Mission San Rafael Arcángel for 13 of its 17 years.

The missionaries believed that their duty was to spread the Christian religion. They were often kinder and gentler leaders than the soldiers. They truly believed that they were helping the California Indians.

While developing Mission San Rafael Arcángel, Fray Gil and Fray Amorós taught the American Indians to sing Christian songs for church services. They taught them Spanish methods of agriculture, weaving, brickmaking, and other skills. Although the mission system produced many problems between the Spaniards and the California Indians, many positive relationships between friars and Indians were formed at Mission San Rafael Arcángel.

◀ *Neophytes were trained in jobs so they could work in the mission community.*

Building the Mission

Immediately after Fray Sarriá raised the cross for the new *asistencia*, supplies were sent from Missions Dolores, Santa Clara, and San José for the construction of the permanent mission buildings.

Because no one sketched or painted the original buildings at Mission San Rafael Arcángel, we cannot be certain what they looked like. Many years later, the Mexican general, Mariano Vallejo, who would one day take over the mission grounds, was asked to draw a picture of Mission San Rafael from memory. He was 70 years old at the time. The picture he drew showed a two-story adobe mission church with a cross above the entrance. The front of the church had a square window supported by redwood beams. Above that was a triangular window to allow air into the granary, where grain was stored.

Under Fray Gil's direction, the neophytes raised an adobe building next to the church. Adobe was used because it kept the building cool in the summer and warm in the winter. This made it a good building material for the missions.

Along the side of the building was a corridor covered with tule, a reed that is native to California. Ten columns supported this corridor. The building was roofed with red tiles.

The mission's tiled roof.

The inside of the church at Mission San Rafael Arcángel.

The Mission Buildings

The mission complex was made up of a hospital, a chapel, a storeroom, and a *monjerío* to house unmarried women and girls. Married women lived with their families in the *ranchería*, in homes that were built outside of the mission buildings. Mission San Rafael Arcángel also had a cemetery, guardhouse, and orchards.

The chapel and other mission buildings at Mission San Rafael Arcángel were very plain. They did not have the beautiful ornaments, designs, or paintings that could be found at the other missions. Unlike other mission buildings, Mission San Rafael Arcángel's church had no tower. The bells were hung in a group from crossbeams in front of the chapel entrance.

Bells at the mission called people to work or prayer.

Mission Bells

Bells were very important at the missions. They not only made a beautiful sound, but their ringing alerted everyone when it was time to be at work or prayer. One of the bells at Mission San Rafael came from an American whale ship. (You can still see the bells at the mission today. They have been preserved as a reminder of the way life was at the mission long ago.) The neophyte boys loved to ring the bells and were told to do so on important occasions, such as when a baby was baptized or when a friar from another mission came to visit.

The mission buildings at Mission San Rafael Arcángel never followed the traditional quadrangle shape of the other missions. As the community grew, Fray Amorós added workshops, granaries, and corrals to fence in the livestock.

This is a painting of the old church at Mission San Rafael.

Daily Life at the Mission

Meals and Prayers

Each day, everyone at the mission, except the sick, woke up at dawn to go to Mass. Afterward, they ate breakfast. They drank hot chocolate and ate *atole. Atole,* or cooked ground corn, was always served at mealtimes. Breakfast was followed by morning chores, such as tending the livestock, grinding meal, or cleaning up.

Between 11:00 A.M. and noon, a midday meal was eaten. The neophytes prepared the meals. Sometimes they served the *atole* with a side dish of mutton or beans. They gave milk to the old and sick.

Work

The men spent the rest of the day working in the fields. They herded the cattle, horses, and sheep. When the harvest season was over, they made adobe bricks from soil mixed with water and straw or made tiles from clay.

Inside their quarters, the women weaved. They produced all the cloth used at the mission, including

▲ *Adobe bricks were used for building.*

blankets, sheets, tablecloths, towels, and napkins. The friars in charge even put in a request for more sheep to be sent from other missions.

◀ *Neophytes worked hard in the mission's fields.*

They explained that the people of Mission San Rafael Arcángel could not dress properly because they needed more wool. More sheep were sent to them.

Work stopped for *siesta* (a period of rest) and began again around 2:00 P.M. During the hot summer afternoons, a burro would carry buckets of vinegar and sweet water to the workers in the fields. This was a rare luxury for them.

The end of the workday came at 5:00 P.M., and at 6:00 P.M., the evening meal was eaten. At this time, the neophytes would often add nuts, herbs, and wild berries to their *atole*. They gathered these in large quantities and stored them away. At sundown, everyone marched to the chapel for prayer. There, they sung the Angelus, a Catholic prayer set to music, and an evening blessing was given. Three times a day, at morning, noon, and night, the bells called everyone to recite the Angelus. Angelus is the Latin word for angels. At 8:00 P.M., women went to bed. Men went to bed at 9:00 P.M.

Study

The friars also spent time teaching the neophytes to read and write, not only in Spanish but also in Latin. This was thought to be important, mainly so that they could understand the Bible scriptures. The neophytes also taught the friars to speak the languages of their tribes. The friars heard confession, a Catholic ritual in which a person tells his or her sins to a priest, in the neophytes' own languages.

The government of New Spain wanted all missionaries to learn the American Indian languages, but not everyone was able to follow this rule. Often it was difficult for the friars to learn the many different languages they heard. Fray Sarriá reminded them that it was their duty to try their best.

Saturdays were sometimes workdays, but on Sundays and holidays, everyone was allowed to rest and play after a few

Mission Indians enjoyed their free time.

hours of prayer. The Catholic religion has many patron saints, and the mission observed the holidays in honor of each saint. The Feast of Saint Raphael was celebrated on October 24. Later, under Mexican rule, October 24 became Rodeo Day. Men would show off their skills on horseback and there would be a bullfight. The last bullfight in San Rafael was in 1870.

Sunday was also a day for trading. California Indians from the surrounding area would come to Mission San Rafael Arcángel to trade. In time, some of them converted and came to live at the mission.

Games

In their free time, the Ohlone Indians played different games, using

▲
The Indians had many games they liked to play.

their hands, sticks, or hoops and poles. In one game for two players, one player would throw a few sticks up in the air. Both players would guess whether the number of sticks was odd or even. A third person would count to see who had guessed right. The loser would pay white shells to the winner. Beads were also sometimes given as prizes.

The lives of neophyte boys and girls at the mission were very different. At around age eight, the girls had to leave their mothers and live and work at the *monjerío*. Once they finished their work, they were allowed to visit their families. At night, they were locked inside. Girls had to live at the *monjerío* under strict supervision until they were married in church and could live in the *ranchería* with their husbands.

Neophyte boys were not locked in at night nor were they forced to stay in during the day. The friars trained the boys to become bell ringers, to sing in the choir, to play the violin, or to be servants.

The Coast Miwok and Ohlone Indians lived an orderly life at the mission, but it was very different from the life they had once known.

Their cultures were changed forever. When the first missionaries came, the American Indians could not foresee that they would lose their freedom, be forced to give up their way of life, and be kept inside the missions.

Many neophytes tried to run away from the missions, but the soldiers went after them and brought them back. The soldiers often treated runaway neophytes with cruelty and punished them with whippings or beatings. Although such punishments were not uncommon Spanish practice at the time, many friars did not like the soldiers to use them on the Indians.

Soldiers were harsh at times.

Life at Mission San Rafael Arcángel was full of challenges for both the missionaries and the neophytes. While the friars were often good men who believed that they were helping the California Indians, the Miwoks and Ohlones found that they were forced to adapt to European beliefs and traditions. In doing so, they lost many of their traditions and ways of life.

Revolt and Revolution at San Rafael

Conflict Between Cultures

As with the other missions, there was some conflict between cultures at Mission San Rafael Arcángel. The Spaniards' way of life and the California Indians' way of life were very different, and the mission system forced the cultures together in a way that, in many cases, was damaging to the Indians' culture. At that time in history, countries colonized new lands to expand their own country's power and wealth even if another people were already settled on that land.

Today, we understand that colonization is an unfair practice that unjustly takes land and liberty away from people. The Spanish missionaries and soldiers thought they were doing a good thing by sharing their religion and lifestyle with the California Indians. We realize today that it is unfair to assume that one culture is superior to, or better than, another culture. Looking back on the mission system, we can see that, in spite of its good intentions, it was unfair for many Indians. It forced them to give up their culture and values, and it was a violation of their civil rights.

While we can look back at historical events today and see the injustice, it was not so easy to see those things at the time when the Spaniards were settling in early California. Some of the California Indians adapted to the new way of life the Spaniards brought, but many others did not want to accept these changes. Many who felt this way were nonetheless forced to stay at the missions and give up their old way of life. There were some who felt more and more hopeless. Others tried to run away. Still others took a different kind of action.

Sometimes California Indians attacked the missions. Fray Amorós

The conflict of cultures sometimes resulted in violence at the missions.

A famous American Indian leader known as Marin made a name for himself by winning many fights against his Spanish enemies. He and another American Indian leader, Quentin, resisted Spanish control of their people. One of the places they attacked was Mission San Rafael Arcángel. Their names were later given to Marin County and San Quentin.

Marin was caught by the soldiers, but the friars at Mission San Rafael Arcángel stopped them from putting him to death. Quentin was also captured after a battle just south of the mission. In the end, Marin was converted to Christianity. Four years later, he was working as a ferry man in San Francisco Bay. He was one of the area's first entrepreneurs. He was given the name Marin because of his talents as a sailor. He died a respected old man and was buried at Mission San Rafael Arcángel.

was always very watchful of attacks by the Indians. He put guards on the lookout all the time.

During one attack, Fray Amorós was saved from harm by the neophytes. They took him to a hiding place and, to protect him, formed a human wall around him. Since the first arrival of the Spaniards, there were some California Indians who welcomed the outsiders and some who did not. The California Indians who wanted to end the mission system fought against the Indians who liked the friars. When the attack finally ended, the survivors, including Fray Amorós, returned to Mission San Rafael Arcángel. They discovered that some things had been stolen and some damage done to the mission. Fray Amorós and the neophytes began the task of cleaning up.

A California Indian named Pomponio, who came from the area of Mission San Rafael Arcángel, raided the countryside as far south as Mission Santa Cruz. He left a trail of robberies, fights, and murders. The violence was usually directed against other Indians. He was finally captured when he killed a white soldier.

In spite of its successes, Mission San Rafael Arcángel's importance was always questioned by the church leaders. In 1823, a plan to convert more of northern California called for both Missions San Rafael Arcángel and Dolores to be closed. It was thought that a "new San Francisco" should be built instead at nearby Sonoma. Fray Amorós worked hard to defend his mission from this threat.

Because of Fray Sarriá's influence, Mission San Rafael Arcángel's destruction was delayed. To help hold off the mission's destruction, 92 neophytes from Mission San Rafael Arcángel had to be transferred to the new community at Sonoma. As always, the neophytes were treated as commodities, or products, to be traded. This practice was not uncommon at the time. Today, this would be considered a serious and unacceptable violation of people's civil rights.

A Change in Leadership

After Fray Amorós died in 1832, a new senior friar took over the running of Mission San Rafael Arcángel. The new senior friar, Fray José Maria Mercado, was a Zacatecan Indian from Mexico.

Secularization

In 1821, New Spain gained its independence from Spain and was renamed Mexico. California and its missions now belonged to Mexico. Some members of the Mexican government wanted to take the missions away from the Catholic church and take over the mission lands for themselves. In 1834, when control of the missions was taken from the Franciscans, Mission San Rafael Arcángel was the first to be affected. The fact is that when Mission San Rafael Arcángel gained official mission status in 1823, time was already running out for the California mission system.

General Mariano Vallejo

In 1834, the Mexican government secularized the missions. This meant that control of the mission lands was taken from the church and given to the government. Mission San Rafael Arcángel, along with the other 20 missions, was no longer run by the friars. A Mexican general named Mariano Vallejo was sent to take control of the mission.

General Vallejo wanted to own Mission San Rafael Arcángel completely. Fray Mercado was known for his bad temper, and he strongly resisted General Vallejo's attempts to control Mission San Rafael Arcángel. Once, a soldier acted on orders from General Vallejo and arrested a neophyte. Fray Mercado was so angry at the soldier that he used "insulting language" when speaking to him, which was something a friar was not supposed to do. Soon Vallejo heard about Fray Mercado's reputation and wanted to use it against him.

One day, Fray Mercado saw a number of unknown California Indians coming toward the mission. Afraid that they were going to

◀ *General Mariano Vallejo.*

45

attack, he gave guns to the neophytes and ordered them to shoot first. Many unarmed California Indians were wounded, and 21 died.

This act of violence by the inhabitants of the mission gave General Vallejo what he was after—a reason to take control of Mission San Rafael Arcángel. At Vallejo's request, Fray Mercado was charged with a number of crimes. He was also accused of being a troublemaker and drinking too much. He was suspended from mission work for six months. The Mexican government gave Vallejo control over all of the mission's resources. Immediately, he moved all the mission's cattle, as well as equipment, supplies, and even vines and fruit trees, to his own ranches. Mission San Rafael Arcángel was abandoned. He gave the California Indians no other choice but to work for him. As at the missions, the Indians were not paid, and they received nothing for their work but room and board.

The land, which the Catholic church had promised to the neophytes, was instead given or sold to Mexican ranchers. Most of the California Indian neophytes went to work on the ranches where they were treated no better than slaves. Other neophytes left the area to make it on their own and fared well in their newfound freedom. Some even became businessmen and landowners.

C. Ynitia

The most successful American Indian in the San Francisco Bay area was C. Ynitia. He was a Miwok who became a neophyte. When the Mexican government took control of the California missions, he was given a land grant of 8,877 acres. He was the only full Indian in Marin County to get a land grant. He gave the land its Indian name, Olompali, making it one of the few places in Marin County to keep its native name. When the Americans started coming to California from the east, C. Ynitia was clever enough to sell his land to them. At a time when other Indian families were being robbed of their lands, C. Ynitia walked away with his money. His daughters married American men.

In 1834, Mission San Rafael Arcángel was grouped in with the Sonoma and San Francisco presidios and turned into a parish, an area with its own church, led by a pastor.

The Bear Flag Revolt.

The Bear Flag Revolt

American rule in California began officially in 1846 with

▲

The American settlers raised the new Bear Flag.

▲

The Bear Flag flies in California's capital city today.

an uprising called the Bear Flag Revolt. Until 1840, there were only a small number of Americans, or Yankees, in California. Most of them were sailors, traders, or adventurers. After 1840, large numbers of Americans headed west in wagon trains. For several years, these Americans made Mexican leaders in California angry. There were fights between the Americans and the Californios (or California settlers of Mexican descent). Then for 25 days in 1846, Sonoma, just north of San Rafael, became the capital of the independent Republic of California.

A rumor had been spreading that Mexico was planning to throw the Americanos (non-Mexican settlers from the east coast of America) out of California. At dawn on June 14, 1846, 33 heavily armed Americans gathered at the fortress home of General Vallejo. They pounded on the door and demanded that General Vallejo surrender the fortress to them. He welcomed three of them in and, after a meal, they arrested him. Then they raised a new flag, which had a bear, a star, and the words "California Republic" on it. Today, the Bear Flag still flies over the state capitol of California in Sacramento.

Under the command of Captain John C. Fremont, the American forces marched down and took San Rafael. Most of the San Francisco Bay area was also handed over to the Americans. Soon the American navy arrived to claim California for the United States and raised the 28-star American flag over Monterey. On January 13, 1847, peace was declared between the Californios and the Americans under the Stars and Stripes. California was now the property of the United States.

Mission San Rafael Arcángel Today

The mission buildings at Mission San Rafael Arcángel were abandoned and eventually torn down in 1861. At the turn of the century, a postcard was created by a native of San Francisco, Felix Adrian Raynaud. The postcard shows what Raynaud imagined Mission San Rafael to look like. The present replica of the mission buildings was raised in 1949. It is now believed that the replica was based on the image on the postcard.

Today, two star-shaped windows grace the front of the church. The building is made of stone, but from the records kept by the friars, we know that the original church was made of adobe.

Many of the things that made the location so good for Mission San Rafael Arcángel are gone today. There were two small streams that brought fresh water from nearby springs to the mission. Ducks, which once lived in nearby mud flats, were an important source of food. Today, their home has become downtown San Rafael.

▲

Sacred objects are on display at the mission.

Mission San Rafael Arcángel is now a tourist site where people can learn about the mission's history and perhaps attend a service. People can also worship at the parish church next door. Mission San Rafael Arcángel has faced many challenges throughout its history and survived them all. Today, the mission stands as a monument to the complex development of the state of California.

◀ *Mission San Rafael Arcángel today.*

Make Your Own Mission
San Rafael Arcángel

dry lasagna noodles	X-Acto knife (Ask for an adult's help.)	miniature bell
Popsicle sticks	red, brown,	scissors
ruler	white, and black	glue
toothpicks	poster paint	string
green Styrofoam		tape
		thin cardboard

Directions

Step 1. Use a large piece of cardboard as your base. For the front and back of the church, draw the shape below on a piece of cardboard. Cut out your outline.
Repeat this step.

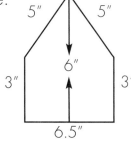

52   Adult supervision is suggested.

Step 2. Cut two pieces of cardboard to measure 3″ by 13″. These will be the sides of the church.

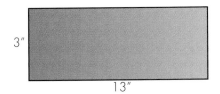

3″

13″

Step 3. Paint all the church walls with white paint. Let dry.

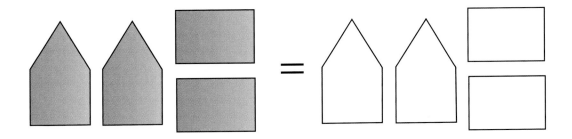

Step 4. To build the friars' quarters, cut two pieces of cardboard to measure 3″ by 12″. These pieces are the front and back.

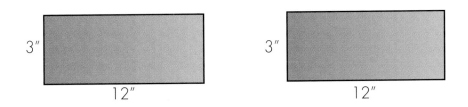

3″

12″

3″

12″

Step 5. Cut two pieces of cardboard to measure 3" by 6.5". These are the sides of the friars' quarters.

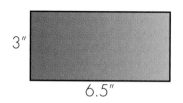

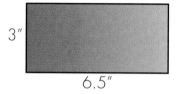

Step 6. Paint the walls of the friars' quarters white. Let dry. Using a pencil, draw where you want doors and windows to be. Do this for the church walls also.

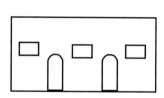

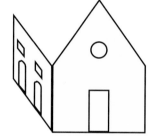

Step 7. Fill in the windows and doors with black paint.

Step 8. Tape the four sides of the church walls together to form a box. Put the tape on the inside, so it doesn't show on the outside of the box.

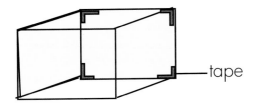

tape

Step 9. Repeat this with the four walls of the friars' quarters to form a box shape.

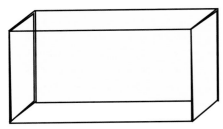

Step 10. Tape both the church and the friars' quarters to your base. Tape the insides only, so the tape doesn't show on the outside.

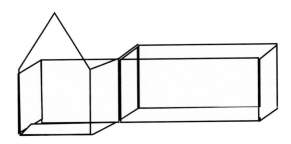

Step 11. To make the roof of the church, cut a piece of cardboard to measure 5" by 14.5". Bend in half and glue to the top of the church walls.

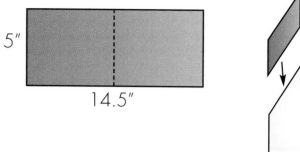

Step 12. For the friars' quarters roof, cut a piece of cardboard 4" by 13". Bend this in half and glue to top of the friars' quarters walls.

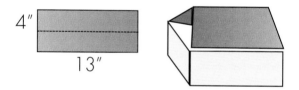

Step 13. Paint lasagna noodles with reddish-brown paint. Let dry. Glue to the roofs.

56

Step 14. Glue 2 toothpicks together to form a cross. Glue to the roof. Decorate the base with green Styrofoam or other greenery. Add crosses to make a cemetery.

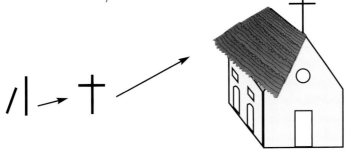

Step 15. Paint Popsicle sticks white. Glue them together as shown below. Tie a string through your miniature bell and hang from Popsicle stick structure. Glue in front of the church.

*Use the above mission as a reference for building your mission.

Important Dates in Mission History

1492	Christopher Columbus reaches the West Indies
1542	Cabrillo's expedition to California
1602	Sebastián Vizcaíno sails to California
1713	Fray Junípero Serra is born
1769	Founding of San Diego de Alcalá
1770	Founding of San Carlos Borromeo del Río Carmelo
1771	Founding of San Antonio de Padua and San Gabriel Arcángel
1772	Founding of San Luis Obispo de Tolosa
1775-76	Founding of San Juan Capistrano
1776	Founding of San Francisco de Asís
1776	Declaration of Independence is signed
1777	Founding of Santa Clara de Asís
1782	Founding of San Buenaventura
1784	Fray Serra dies
1786	Founding of Santa Bárbara
1787	Founding of La Purísima Concepción
1791	Founding of Santa Cruz and Nuestra Señora de la Soledad
1797	Founding of San José, San Juan Bautista, San Miguel Arcángel, and San Fernando Rey de España
1798	Founding of San Luis Rey de Francia
1804	Founding of Santa Inés
1817	**Founding of San Rafael Arcángel**
1823	Founding of San Francisco de Solano
1848	Gold found in northern California
1850	California becomes the 31st state

58

Glossary

adapt (a-DAPT) To become used to something.

adobe (uh-DOH-Bee) Sun-dried bricks made of straw, mud, and sometimes manure.

agriculture (A-grih-kul-cherr) Farming.

baptism (BAP-tih-zum) A ceremony performed when someone is accepted into, or accepts, the Christian faith.

colonization (kah-luh-nih-ZAY-shun) Claiming land already occupied by other people and bringing new settlers to live there.

community (kuh-MYOO-nih-tee) A group of people who live together in the same place.

confession (kon-FEH-shun) A Catholic ritual in which a person tells his or her sins.

convert (kun-VIRT) To cause someone to change a belief.

fertile (FUR-til) Being able to produce plants or crops easily.

Franciscans (fran-SIS-kinz) Members of the Franciscan order, a part of the Catholic church dedicated to preaching, missionaries, and charities.

friar (FRY-ur) A brother in a communal religious order. A friar can also be a priest.

granary (GRAY-nuh-ree) A building where grain is stored.

livestock (LYV-stahk) Animals raised on a farm or ranch.

luxury (LUK-shur-ee) Something that gives comfort or pleasure but is not necessary.

Mass (MAS) The main religious ceremony of some churches, such as the Catholic church.

missionary (MI-shuh-nayr-ee) Someone who is sent to spread his or her religion in another country.

neophyte (NEE-oh-fyt) The name given to a California Indian living at a mission who has converted to the Christian faith.

New World (NOO WURLD) What the Europeans once called the combined areas of North, South, and Central America.

parish (PAR-ish) An area with its own church and minister or priest.

quadrangle (KWAHD-rang-gul) The square at the center of a mission that is surrounded by four buildings.

replica (REH-plih-cah) A copy of something that looks just like the original.

resource (REE-sors) The wealth of a place.

restoration (rehs-tuh-RAY-shun) Working to return something, like a building, to its original state.

secularization (seh-kyuh-luh-rih-ZAY-shun) A process by which something, such as a mission, is made to be non-religious.

settlement (SEH-tuhl-ment) A small village or group of houses.

territory (TEHR-ih-tor-ee) A big area of land.

tule (TOO-lee) A reed used by the California Indians to make houses and boats.

Pronunciation Guide

asistencias (a-sis-TEN-see-uhs)

atole (ah-TOL-ay)

fray (FRAY)

monjerío (mohn-HAYR-ee-oh)

rancherías (RAHN-cher-EE-as)

siesta (see-EHS-tah)

temescal (TEH-mes-cal)

Resources

To learn more about the missions of California, check out these books and Web sites and this video:

Books

Genet, Donna. *Father Junípero Serra: Founder of the California Missions.* Springfield, NJ: Enslow Publishers, 1996.

Keyworth, C.L. *The First Americans: California Indians.* New York, New York: Facts on File, 1991.

Van Steenwyk, Elizabeth. *The California Missions.* New York, NY: Franklin Watts, 1995.

Young, Stanley. *The Missions of California.* San Francisco, CA: Chronicle Books, 1998.

Web Sites

http://www.ca-mission.org/links.html

http://www.cucq.k12.ca.us/lessons/missions/contents/index.html

http://www.escusd.k12.ca.us/MissionTrail.html

Video

California Missions. Huell Howser Productions/funded by Mervyns California. (California Missions #107: San Francisco de Asís, **San Rafael Arcángel**, San Francisco de Solano.)

Index